THE GIRL WHO WORE HER HEART ON HER BACK

By:

Dr. Ravin Ellis, PharmD

Scriptures marked KJV are taken from the KING JAMES VERSION (KJV): KING JAMES VERSION, public domain.

Scripture quotations marked (NLT) are taken from the Holy Bible, New Living Translation, copyright ©1996, 2004, 2015 by Tyndale House Foundation. Used by permission of Tyndale House Publishers, Carol Stream, Illinois 60188. All rights reserved.

Copyright © 2021 by Dr. Ravin M. Ellis, PharmD, RHIA

All rights reserved. No part of this book may be reproduced or used in any manner without written permission of the copyright owner except for the use of quotations in a book review. For more information, address: drravinpharmd@gmail.com

FIRST EDITION

www.drravinpharmd.com

This book is dedicated to my beautiful children,
Kyron, my angel in heaven
Kylie, my beautiful princess
Christian, my handsome prince
Marysa, my first angel
Know that I love you all with everything that's in me, and there's nothing that will ever stop your mother's love.

Table of Contents

Introduction 1
Chapter One 3
    IT'S OKAY TO CRY 3
Chapter Two 9
    IT'S OKAY TO FEEL 9
Chapter Three 14
    IT'S OKAY TO BE YOU 14
Chapter Four 20
    IT'S OKAY TO BE DIFFERENT 20
Chapter Five 26
    IT'S OKAY TO GRIEVE 26
Chapter Six 32
    IT'S OKAY TO LOVE AGAIN 32
Chapter Seven 39
    IT'S OKAY TO LIVE 39

Introduction

I've heard the phrase "wearing your heart on your sleeve" several times in my life. If you ask an average person what the phrase means, I'm sure they would tell you that the person is emotional or shows emotion often. That person expresses himself or herself in a way that others know exactly what he or she is feeling in the moment. Well, I am that person. However, when God created me, He threw in a bit of a twist.

> *Psalms 139:14 (NKJV) I will praise You, for I am fearfully and wonderfully made; Marvelous are Your works, and that my soul know very well*

When I was born, there was a mole on my back in the shape of a heart. When I was almost two years old, the mole was removed, leaving a very distinct scar in that same shape. This scar left an everlasting mark on me, shaping the very woman I am today.

It took years before I recognized the significance of the mark that I would bear for the rest of my life. Somehow, I always knew it was meant to stay a part of me. While I was teased and asked if I was burned several times throughout my life, I knew that this scar, this thorn, would reveal who I was meant to be. So, when I was given the opportunity to have it removed at the age of sixteen, I declined. It was one of the best decisions I've ever made in my life. That decision helped me to accept the fact that I am different. I accepted the fact that I am unique, but most of all, I am His. This journey through life has not been easy. I've had some really big highs and really low lows. Through it all, God was right there guiding me through. Through every tear, every scream, every moment that felt like I could go no more, He was there to carry me through. I didn't know it then, but as I am writing right now, it's more evident than ever.

This book is my story. It is my journey through discovering my emotions. It is a chronicle of some of the things I've been through, and the emotions attached to those situations. While I am not my emotions, it is important to recognize that it's okay to have emotions. God wants us to live, feel, trust, cry, grow, and experience all the emotions we do. The key to walking through life is depending on God and turning those emotions over to Him. This allows Him to help you when times are rough and celebrate with you in times of joy.

> *Ecclesiastes 3:1 (NKJV) To everything there is a season,*
> *A time for every purpose under heaven.*

God knows every emotion. He created every detail in us including the capacity to express emotions. He knows that life has ups and downs, trials and tribulations. He also promised that He would never leave us during those times.

At the end of each chapter, take some time to journal your thoughts. I've included space to allow you to write down anything that God reveals to you as you read. I pray that this book blesses you and guides you to a deeper understanding of your God-given emotions. I pray that you see yourself in each chapter and know that it's all okay. I pray that this book ministers to those who feel misunderstood, judged, or closed in for being expressive. Most of all, I pray that God meets you where you are and that you have a supernatural encounter, feeling His overwhelming and everlasting love for you.

Chapter One
IT'S OKAY TO CRY

Have you ever been told you're too emotional or too sensitive? Have you ever been told that you cry too much? Have you ever poured your heart out to someone, and that person criticized you for doing so?

I ask these questions because I've been there. As a child, I was called everything under the sun. I was "whiny" and a "cry baby." Some even called me "Crying Cathy." I was told that all I did was cry. As I look back at that time in my life, my first thought is "why". Why did I cry so much? Why did I express myself through crying? Furthermore, why did the adults around me respond to my tears with frustration and criticism? It would be years before I realized that the tears that I cried were a form of release and quite frankly, a type of prayer.

Cry. The Webster 1913 online dictionary describes the word cry as a verb. It means to make a loud call or cry; to call or exclaim vehemently or earnestly; to shout; to vociferate; to proclaim; to pray; to implore; to utter lamentations; to lament audibly; to express pain, grief, or distress, by weeping and sobbing; to shed tears; to bawl, as a child. Some versions of the word cry or crying appear in 168 verses of the King James Version of the Bible. You may wonder why I give you this information. I spent most of my life believing that something was wrong with me. It wasn't until I accepted my identity in Christ that things began to make sense. I walked around, ignorant of my true identity and self-worth when the truth about me was there all along. As I read the stories in the Bible, I began to see me in more ways than one. For Christians, the Bible is our manual or guide to living the way God intended. Most of us try to live according to the standards our Heavenly Father set for us in the Bible. The numerous mentions of crying in the Bible gave me a sense of peace and a release to allow my tears to flow without remorse.

Psalms 61:1 (NLT) O God, listen to my cry! Hear my prayer!
1 Samuel 1:10 (NLT) Hannah was in deep anguish crying bitterly as she prayed to the Lord

As a follower of Christ, it gives me comfort to know that crying is welcomed by the Father. After years of hearing that I cried too much, I was happy to see that God wants to hear our cries. It's a language that He understands better than we think. When Hannah cried out to God, He answered. When David cried out to God, He answered. These acts were not just a time of "whining." Just as Hannah and David expressed their pain, joys, and sorrows to God through their tears, I learned that I have permission to do so as well. Their cries were the heartfelt expressions that God needed and wanted to hear. God wanted their vulnerability, and He expects the same from us. Our Heavenly Father created us to commune with us, and the vulnerability that comes with crying allows us to have a real relationship with Him.

Proverbs 2:3 (NLT) Cry out for insight and ask for understanding.

Crying is communication. The tears that drop are like words that can only be heard by the intended heart. Like a parent who knows the distinction of the various cries of an infant, God knows the words associated with each tear drop. Your tears are the unspoken requests that reaches God's ears as well as His heart. It took a while to understand that my tears were actually complete sentences. As His daughter, He understood every cry. When I was ready to recognize Him as my Father, I opened the door for Him to respond to each teardrop. It's amazing how He answers a prayer when you haven't uttered a single word. I remember when I gave birth to my first son prematurely. I cried for hours every day. It was hard to accept that my son was fighting for his life, and there was nothing that I could do about it. Even in my ignorance of my authority as His daughter, He still heard my prayers and tears as I sang worship songs to Kyron during NICU visitations.

So, don't stop yourself from communicating through your tears. Release the sound that sets you free from the pressure and stress. Release the tears that speak to the matters of your heart. Do not allow anyone to stifle the voice attached to your tears. Do not allow the stigma of sensitivity to make you think you are weak. There is strength and freedom in your tears, in the wail of your cries. The ability to cry and be vulnerable in the presence of others shows the courage within you. If you ask me, there's nothing weak about that.

I have experienced many things in life that made me cry, and I'll talk about some of those experiences later in the book. There were times when I tried to hold in my tears to appear to be strong. I tried to avoid the names I heard as a child. I would soon realize that everything that I held in was a weight pulling me down, deeper into depression. Once I finally allowed myself to release all that was built up, the tears I shed led to the beginning of the true healing I needed. I realized that crying opened the door to healing instead of blocking it. By allowing myself to cry when needed, I released the heaviness and weight.

> [Psa 55:22 KJV] 22 Cast thy burden upon the LORD, and he shall sustain thee: he shall never suffer the righteous to be moved.

Allow God to take the weight that you've been carrying all along. I know it's easier said than done. It took a while for me to release it all and give it to Him. I still find it hard at times because I've been so accustomed to carrying it all. I still try to save face and hold in the tears from time to time. Then I remember that crying is not a bad thing as long as I give my tears to the One who created them. I allow Him to carry the weight.

REFLECTION

Chapter Two

IT'S OKAY TO FEEL

Feel. It means to have perception by the touch, or by contact of anything with the nerves of sensation, especially those upon the surface of the body; to have the sensibilities moved or affected; to be conscious of an inward impression, state of mind, persuasion, physical condition, etc.; to perceive oneself to be to know with feeling; to be conscious; hence, to know certainly or without misgiving.

Feelings. Just the definition of the word feel by the online 1913 Webster Dictionary seems a bit overwhelming. The definition ranges from the physical to the mind. The way that we view feelings determines the way that we deal with them. Often, people try to avoid feelings because they have been taught that they are negative. "Feelings are fickle." Have you heard that one before? While that may be true, feelings are more than that. Yes, how you feel may change frequently. Sometimes, our feelings are simply out of control. However, they serve a purpose. Now, you may ask, "What is the purpose of our feelings?" My response is everything that follows this next scripture. Just keep reading. I promise I'm getting to the point.

> *Then God said, "Let us make human beings in our image, to be like us. They will reign over the fish in the sea, the birds in the sky, the livestock, all the wild animals on the earth, and the small animals that scurry along the ground." So, God created human beings in his own image. In the image of God, he created them; male and female he created them. Genesis 1:26-27 (NLT)*

God made us in His image to be like Him. So, not only do we have the love, power, and peace that He has given us through the Holy Spirit, but we also have the capacity to feel the same way He does. It took time for me to realize that it was okay to feel what I was feeling. It took time to realize that it was okay to express what was on my heart. It took years for me to realize that I looked like Him. Once I accepted my identity in Him, I accepted the parts of me that came from Him. That acceptance included my feelings.

It's hard to think of feelings as a positive thing when so many people tell us that they are negative. People speak of them as if they are a plague that no one should ever expose to the world. The fact is that feelings come from God. He designed us to feel because He feels. There are several scriptures in the Bible where God clearly shows emotion. While God expresses His feelings towards His creations, He also gives us the blueprint to handling those feelings.

O Lord don't rebuke me in your anger or discipline me in your rage! (Ps. 38:1 NLT)

This scripture speaks of the anger displayed by God when His people disobeyed Him. It's not the only scripture that shows us that God felt angry at the choices made by His chosen people. However, God did not stay angry with us, just as He expects us not to stay angry.

And "don't sin by letting anger control you." Don't let the sun go down while you are still angry (Eph 4:26 NLT)

While it is clear that God recognizes that we will feel anger, He encourages us not to stay angry. Think about that. God never said that we cannot feel what He feels. He knows exactly how He created us. However, He encourages us to not remain in those feelings so that we do not sin. This is where feelings become complicated. When we allow ourselves to overthink what we're feeling, it opens the door to sin. Instead of marinating on it, God encourages us to hand that feeling over to Him and allow Him to work on us through it.

Feelings. They can be good or bad. While the Father has given us feelings to navigate through life, He has also given us free will. That means that we decide what we do with our feelings. It is how we choose to express our feelings that determine the effect of them on our lives. You may choose to hold onto your sadness or anger without saying a word to the person who triggered that emotion. While that may appear to be the peacemaker approach, it creates the opportunity for that emotion to become something that leads to sin. I found myself doing this often with family members and friends. I can remember the lingering thought of "blessed be the peacemaker." I truly believe that many Christians take this approach because they believe that's how God wants us to be. However, even Jesus flipped a table and spoke the truth. Jesus confronted the issue at hand. I'm not saying that flipping tables wherever you go is the answer. I am saying that confronting the issue related to your feelings is okay. In fact, it is suggested as long as it is done in a healthy way. Just remember this………you were made in His image. If God expresses His feelings towards us, why can't you?

REFLECTION

Chapter Three
IT'S OKAY TO BE YOU

A uthentic. The word is defined as having a genuine original or authority, in opposition to that which is false, fictitious, counterfeit, or apocryphal; being what it purports to be; genuine; not of doubtful origin; real; authoritative; of approved authority; true; trustworthy; credible; as, an authentic writer; an authentic portrait; authentic information. We often hear people speak of keeping it 100 or keeping it real. However, it's hard to keep it real with others when we are not real with ourselves. So, I have a few questions for you.

Do you know the REAL you?
Are you who God created you to be?
Do you know what you're called to do?

These seem like simple questions. However, take some time to really think about the real you. I encourage you to spend an evening alone with God and a journal. During your time alone, ask God the hard questions about yourself. I'm not talking about the surface level questions that we hear when meeting someone for the first time. I'm talking about real, honest, deep, thought-provoking questions. These questions are uncomfortable when you're not being true to yourself. Well, I'm here to say that it's okay to be you and to find out exactly who you are.

Thank you for making me so wonderfully complex! Your workmanship is marvelous-how well I know it (Psalms 139:14 NLT)

When I was growing up, I wasn't happy with me. I especially wasn't happy with my appearance. I had this massive scar on my neck and back from the surgical removal of a mole called a congenital pigmented nevus. My skin was darker than most of the kids in my class. To top it off, my name was RAVEN (imagine the big black, annoying bird in The Wiz). Oh, I can't forget that I was one of the smarter kids in the class, i.e., the nerd. Needless to say, this combination led to bullying. Some kids teased me about my scar, my skin color, and even my name. It was so bad that I convinced my mother to legally change my name to RAVIN. Somehow, in my 7-year-old mind, I was convinced that changing the spelling of my name would keep the kids from teasing me. I had long hair, so I often tried to wear my hair down so that no one would see the scar on my neck. I tried to change or hide everything about me that made me, well, me.

Years passed before I became comfortable in the skin I walked in. I remember that transition occurred in high school. I went to an all-girl high school, and it was amazing to see so many young women walking around absolutely loving themselves. In fact, the school encouraged it. It was at Xavier University Preparatory School that I started to acknowledge just how wonderfully made I was.

Sophomore year, I made the cheerleading team. The summer after that year, I was given the opportunity to have the scar that I lived with my entire life removed. I remember going to the appointment with the plastic surgeon at Ochsner Hospital. The doctor explained the lengthy process that included balloons being placed under my skin to expand the skin. The extra skin that grew would then be folded over the scar to create one thin line down my back instead of the massive scar that I had been living with. For the first time, I chose not to hide something that was a part of me. I declined the surgery. It was then that I truly started to live in my authentic self. That was just the beginning for me. A confidence grew within me that shocked even my mother. She was so surprised when I chose to wear a halter top dress for my senior prom. I also wore my hair pinned up. Finally, I began to see my physical beauty that God created despite the scar. It would be years before I recognized the beauty within.

As I look back on the years of my life and the trials, I realize that I often tried to change the person who God created so that I would fit in with everyone else. I was seeking approval most of my life, and I didn't realize it. While being smart was the one thing I truly identified with, I had no idea who I really was until recently. It took going through two divorces, the loss of more than one job, the loss of my son, the loss of my finances, several breaks from toxic relationships, and moving several times for me to see that I was trying to adjust to the ideas of who and what I should be instead of embracing who God called me to be.

Of course, the innate characteristics that were true to who I am remained a part of me. However, the layers that I added on throughout the years to avoid rejection, abandonment, and disappointment began to fade away. Through the help of the leaders at Emmanuel Kingdom Fellowship and my close friends, I began to break through the issues that laid one on top of the other, to create a hard impenetrable shell that had continued to grow through each trauma I experienced. My leaders pointed me back to God. As I write this book, I am still in the process of working through this shell that I created. It's no longer impenetrable because Jesus broke the outer layer. As I pray and spend time with Him, another layer is removed, revealing more of the woman I am meant to be. Now, I embrace my quirks, my skin, my scar, and my name in totality. Now, I'm okay with simply being me.

REFLECTION

Chapter Four

IT'S OKAY TO BE DIFFERENT

Different. The 1913 Webster's online dictionary defines different as distinct; separate; not the same; other; of various or contrary nature, form, or quality; partially or totally unlike; dissimilar; as, different kinds of food or drink; different states of health; different shapes; different degrees of excellence. If I could insert a praise dance in this chapter, I would! Let me explain.

The previous chapter spoke about accepting who you are as God's perfect masterpiece. Some of the things I listed in the previous chapter were things that made me different. It was hard to accept those differences growing up, especially because they were differences that I could not hide. They stood out, and I couldn't run away from them. This chapter challenges you to embrace your differences. Not only do these characteristics, whether physical or not, make you who you are; they also SET YOU APART!

> [Jer 1:5 NLT] "I knew you before I formed you in your mother's womb. Before you were born I set you apart and appointed you as my prophet to the nations."

Almost two years ago, a good friend of mine gave me a housewarming gift when I moved into a new apartment. I was settling into my apartment after downsizing yet again. However, this move was different. During this move, God stripped away all the old things I was carrying with me over the years. I went through a purging season where I gave away and sold everything that tied me to the old me after truly giving my life to Christ. In place of the old things, God made sure that I purchased new and inexpensive furniture as well as little things here and there. Let's just say that the décor was not the most elaborate for this two-bedroom apartment. However, the gift that my friend gave me reminded me of everything I experienced and who God called me to be. The 16 x 24 sized canvas, framed in wood simply said, "before you were born I set you apart." I stared at those words repeatedly for quite a while before I hung it on the wall. As I looked back over my life, I tried to understand where and how was I set apart. In that apartment, I finally understood what it meant.

So, what sets me apart? Let's address the biggest thing first. The scar. I explained in the previous chapter that the scar on my neck and back came from a mole at birth that formed the shape of a heart. Where have you seen that before? I think God really knocked it out the park when He designed that one. As painful as it was to be teased by other children, deep down inside, I knew that my scar made me different. It took years for me to accept it, but God knew exactly what He was doing when He formed me. If you ask some of my friends, they will tell you that I have a big heart. I have a heart for people and love to help in any way possible. Helping others is why I became a pharmacist. Well, I later realized that I not only had a big heart, but I also had an extra one. Of course, the one on my back would be God's art, His perfect masterpiece. Every masterpiece deserves a spotlight, right? If you haven't realized it by now, my heart on my back graces the cover of this book.

> *[1Ki 17:6 NIV] 6 The ravens brought him bread and meat in the morning and bread and meat in the evening, and he drank from the brook.*

As if the masterpiece on my back wasn't enough, my name has been a conversation starter over the years. I mentioned in the previous chapter that I was teased for having the name of a black bird in elementary school. This prompted a name change from R-A-V-E-N to R-A-V-I-N. Changing the spelling of my name helped a little, but not much. Instead, my name was mispronounced often throughout the years. I also remember reciting Edgar Allan Poe's "The Raven" more times than I ever wanted. When stating my name over the years, I often heard "that's different." In response, I would simply tell them that my name is like the black bird with an I instead of an E. I didn't realize how special my name was until I joined a Christian mentorship program for women. One group session led me on a journey of exploring my name. As I looked in the dictionary and the Bible, I realized that the original spelling was the one with the meaning. Furthermore, the raven in the Bible was a bird with purpose. In the Bible, the raven was a messenger and a caregiver. The light bulbs went off when I realized that God gave me a name that matched my purpose. Just as the ravens cared for Elijah, I have cared for many people in many ways. I've cared for my children from difficult pregnancies to my oldest son taking his last breath. I've cared for numerous patients over my 20 years as a pharmacist, informing and guiding patients in healthcare. I've even been the messenger as I've shared information and encouragement when needed. It was in that moment that I realized that even my name set me apart.

Distinct. Diverse. Nonidentical. Unalike.

No matter which word you choose, choose to be exactly who God has called you to be. Being different is not easy because we are so accustomed to fitting in. We find ourselves wanting to blend in so that we are accepted. That's exactly what I wanted. I wanted to be accepted by the children I went to school with. I wanted their approval. I wanted to be liked by everyone. The problem with needing the approval of others is that the cycle never ends. I constantly found myself doing things that I didn't normally do just to "prove" myself to others who didn't even care about me. Eventually, I lost myself trying to become someone different. Look at that. There's that word different again. If only I knew that my "different" was enough.

It's hard learning to embrace who you are when you don't know who you are. As I entered my adolescent years, I began to see just a glimpse of who I was meant to be. There was this desire in me to help others and encourage others to succeed. There was a sadness that came over me when I saw people miss the mark or even fail. I saw the best in people, and I still do. Now that I know who I am in Christ, I have embraced every single part of me. I've embraced my differences that allow me to live according to God's plan for me. I'm not perfect, and that's the best part. I'm not perfect; I'm different...distinct...nonidentical...unalike...unapologetically and unashamedly RAVIN.

REFLECTION

Chapter Five

IT'S OKAY TO GRIEVE

Grieve. The 1913 Webster's online dictionary defines grieve as to occasion grief to; to wound the sensibilities of; to make sorrowful; to cause to suffer; to afflict; to hurt; to try; to sorrow over; as, to grieve one's fate; to feel grief; to be in pain of mind on account of an evil; to sorrow; to mourn; -- often followed by at, for, or over. It's a word that no one ever wants to discuss. It's also the word that I have experienced over and over again. Well, I actually didn't grieve as many times as I should have throughout the years. I'll explain later.

[Ecc 3:4 NLT] 4 A time to cry and a time to laugh. A time to grieve and a time to dance.

When I look back over the years, I realize that grieving was something I found hard to do. It's interesting. As the emotional being that I have been over the years, I've never had a problem with crying or showing emotion. I realized that as an adult, however, I did have a problem with grieving. Here's the thing that some people don't realize. Crying isn't equal to grieving. Crying may be a manifestation of grieving, but the appearance of tears does not always indicate proper grieving. I recently discovered that I have never properly grieved every loss that I have suffered, and there have been a lot of losses. So, the question is "what was I doing all those years with all those tears?" That's a really good question.

Throughout the years I have lost a lot. The loss that stood out the most was, of course, the death of my son when he was 17. I also suffered a miscarriage and buried a stillborn. Each of my children were high risk pregnancies, causing me to lose the joyful experience of being pregnant. I endured two divorces over the span of 7 years. If those weren't enough, there were a few more uncommon losses that happened in my 43 years. Many don't think of losing a job as a true loss. Well, I lost two jobs over the years, which meant losing stability. It meant losing longevity in my career. It meant losing status in my profession. This ultimately meant losing income. It doesn't stop there. Losing income meant losing a home and embracing apartment living. Let's keep going... I lost relationships too. My daughter moved in with her father. Because of our strained relationship, I missed her high school years. My best friend of over 30 years was no longer my best friend. Relationships within my family became rocky. Of all the loss that I suffered, I never truly allowed myself to grieve.

I know you're wondering how I didn't grieve after all of that. As each life changing event happened in my life, I suppressed what I was feeling and covered it up with everything that I could find. It became a routine to escape the grief through some other source. During my first marriage, instead of dealing with the several levels of loss, I threw myself into working long hours that led me to focus on everything instead of life at home. I was in a relationship that was failing, and I didn't want to face that because failure isn't perfection. I was still dealing with the fact of feeling less than a woman because I didn't experience the typical full-term pregnancy. Through all the hurt that I was feeling, I wasn't feeling at all. Instead of allowing myself to feel the pain and grieve, I covered it all up becoming this person that I wasn't. Who did I become? I became an arrogant, overachieving, workaholic, picture of perfection. The woman who was once loving, giving, sensitive, and eager to help anyone began to slowly shut down and build walls that blocked everything out. This is what happens when we don't allow ourselves to process the things that happen in life. I didn't allow myself to grieve the lack of a normal pregnancy. I didn't allow myself to grieve even not having a "normal" son due to his very premature birth. I kept pushing through all of it because I thought that's what strength and perfection looked like. Well, I was wrong. Over the years, I experienced more loss.

Of all the experiences, losing my son was the greatest. It was the ultimate loss that set me on a spiral of emotions, leading me to behave in ways that I would never have imagined. I chose to "be strong" for my children and my family. I remember Facebook posts and messages from friends and family telling me how they admired my strength. I often replied that it wasn't my strength that they saw; it was God's strength. As I look back on it now, it was God's grace and mercy. My appearance of strength was a mere illusion of what was really going on inside. I began to live as if there was no tomorrow and consequently, making decisions that were not a reflection of who God created. I sinned and hurt others because I was hurting. This was all because I didn't take the time to grieve yet again, and I didn't take my grief to God.

I remember the day of my son's wake. It would be my first time seeing my son in the casket, realizing that he wouldn't come home from the hospital as he'd done so many times before. I stared at him. He was becoming a young man and had a mustache. When I looked into that casket, I saw the young man that I was raising. I didn't see my baby boy. I saw a young man. It was the first time that I saw him, knowing that he wouldn't need my help. Even in realizing who I was losing in that moment, I didn't cry. The one time that I should've cried, kicked, screamed, hollered, and acted a complete fool, I didn't. I just stared. It didn't end there. I continued to push through the grief year after year instead of dealing with the reality of all that I lost.

If I continued to talk about every single thing I lost, this chapter would be longer than the book. I could go on and on about how I responded to the things that happened in my life instead of embracing the loss. The scripture I quoted at the beginning of this chapter says that there is a time to cry and a time to laugh, but there's also a time to grieve. Allowing yourself to grieve means taking the time to process how you feel about what you've lost. It means giving yourself permission to be mad, sad, or whatever you're feeling in the moment. It means being okay with telling God exactly how you're feeling and knowing that He hears every word of it. It means letting go of what was, in order to embrace the new things, situations, or people in your life.

Grieving is a process. It takes time, and it's hard. That's the reality of it. However, I thank God for the healing process. There is freedom and strength that comes with it. As you let go of the pain, you begin to realize that you can make it through. Life is not over. That's the beauty of grief. Once I finally gave it to God and started working through it all, He began to break down the walls that held me captive. Brick by brick, the wall is still coming down. Brick by brick, light is shining through. Step by step, God is revealing the new me that He is molding. Will I ever forget the experiences of loss? No. I could never forget. I don't want to forget, especially my son. However, the more I allow God to heal those hidden parts of me, the easier it gets to embrace my future. Please allow yourself to grieve so that you may truly live the life God has for you.

REFLECTION

Chapter Six

IT'S OKAY TO LOVE AGAIN

LOVE. The word is defined as a feeling of strong attachment induced by that which delights or commands admiration; preeminent kindness or devotion to another; affection; tenderness; as, the love of brothers and sisters. The word appears in the King James version of the Bible 310 times. Love is just that important to God. After all, the most famous scripture of the Bible says exactly that.

> [Jhn 3:16 KJV] 16 For God so loved the world, that he gave his only begotten Son, that whosoever believeth in him should not perish, but have everlasting life.

When I think of what love represented when I was younger, I thought about relationships, boyfriends, girlfriends, and the mushy stuff I saw on television. I was in love with the idea of love at an early age. So, when the opportunity came for me to express love, it was easy. I was the girl who fell in "love" quickly with every boyfriend. I was the one who always said it first and was crushed when I didn't hear it said back to me. I was affectionate and not afraid to show my love. Well, I also learned at an early age that love was hard and complicated. Contrary to what I saw on television, love was not a simple thing. Most movies focused on love seemed to have the same theme. Love was this beautiful thing that gave you instant butterflies the moment you saw the one you thought you were meant to be with for the rest of your life. The birds chirped. The sun shined brighter than any other day. Your eyes met, and you instantly knew that this moment was meant to be. Well, love doesn't quite work like that. It took a long time to learn that real love is a choice.

Over the years, I learned a lot about real love through my two marriages. I got married the first time at a really young age. I was 19, and he was 20. Our son was a year old, and we were living together by the time we decided to get married in an early Friday morning ceremony at his childhood church. I remember wearing a simple white prom dress purchased at Macy's with my best friend's discount. It was a short ceremony with very few people in attendance. In fact, my mother was out of town that day. My father walked me down the aisle and in just a few minutes, I became a wife for the first time.

We were married for 9 years before getting a divorce. Those 9 years had many ups and downs, but each moment taught me about what real love looked like. Real love required two people coming together before God and making a commitment to truly endure all the circumstances that would be thrown at them. Real love was not throwing in the towel but rising to the occasion and fighting. I'm not saying that we didn't love each other. We did in our own way. However, we lost faith. We lost hope, and I lost myself amid a marriage that tested me.

> [1Co 13:7 NLT] 7 Love never gives up, never loses faith, is always hopeful, and endures through every circumstance.

When I look back over that marriage, I realized that God was not the center of it. We were both in the marriage, doing the things that married people do. We were living a life that indicated that we were married. We built a couple of houses, bought a couple of cars, had another child, and moved to Texas in those nine years. We checked off the boxes from the outside looking in, but marriage is a covenant. When we said our vows, we made a covenant before God. However, we didn't include God in our marriage like we should have. We didn't make him the foundation of our union. How could we have truly loved each other when the ONE who is love wasn't present in our marriage?

We tried so many times to make Him apart of our union. We changed churches a few times. He even looked into becoming Catholic because Catholic services allowed me to still go to church and work on the weekend. Eventually, we got to a place of not attending church on a regular basis. It's not surprising that we never got to a place in our relationship where God was more important than the things we were dealing with in life. Crazy work schedules, arguments about the roles we played, a disabled child who demanded time and attention, a toddler who demanded time and attention, and external family demands all led to the downfall of our marriage. Nine long years. Every relationship has trials and tribulations, but those relationships that include God in every aspect of life and love are the ones who make it through. I realized that AFTER the divorce. Unfortunately, the damage was done, and the pain set in as I moved on searching for someone to simply love me for me.

I met my next husband the same year of my divorce from my first husband. I was broken and hurting. I wanted someone to love me for me, and I was looking in all the wrong places. The fact that I was looking is an entirely different discussion. I met him at my brother's graduation party, and I was drawn to the way he walked with my son. My late son, Kyron, was blind and known for wanting to walk all the time. So, when he walked with Kyron after everyone else had their turn, I saw someone that was capable of love. That night began a story of ups and downs yet again. After one year of an off and on situationship, he came to live with me and my children. I know that situationship is not a word, but that's exactly what it was until I took him in. I was still functioning from a broken place, knowing that my ex-husband had moved on with his then fiancé. So, I chose this man to fill a void, a love that only God could fill.

We immediately began to play the role of husband and wife without the ring or God in the middle. We got pregnant within 4 months of living together. I was excited because I always wanted a third child, and this was an opportunity to redeem the other pregnancies. In my mind, it would all be different. Unfortunately, God had other plans as my daughter, Marysa Nicole Ellis, was a stillborn at 22 weeks of pregnancy. Immediately after burying my daughter, I expressed to my then boyfriend, that I would not "shack up" longer than 2 years. In my mind, if he didn't marry me by then, he never would. There was no proposal, just an agreement to plan a wedding. Again, God was not involved in any of these decisions, and I just wanted to be loved.

During the time that we planned the wedding, my "fiancé" began to have some experiences that he claimed were encounters with God. The one thing I remember telling him was "God is love, and you're not leading us in love." We were going to church more consistently before the wedding. We even had one counseling session with my childhood babysitter who was now a pastor and the person who married us. We eventually decided to try to get pregnant again. I thought I would probably end up pregnant after the wedding. I was so wrong. I found out 3 weeks before the wedding that I was pregnant. Things really changed after that wedding.

I learned a lot from the mistakes in my first marriage. This time around, I tried to be the biblical wife, honoring my husband throughout the marriage. I made sure that I didn't make decisions without him, allowing him to lead us. We continued to go to church on most but not all Sundays. We even sought counsel with another minister in Louisiana. He spoke with the minister on a consistent basis, and I spoke with his wife. I kept telling myself that whatever happened, I could not get a divorce again. That would not be the case. The man I married was not the man that God chose for me; I chose him to escape loneliness and heartbreak. I put my family through so much drama trying to make a marriage work that wasn't meant to be. I was trying to be the perfect wife to the wrong person. In my quest to find love, I found heartache and another divorce. After 4 years of marriage, I found myself alone again.

After the second divorce, I told myself that I would wait a while to date again. I convinced myself that I was content with just my children. I didn't need anyone else to "complete me." I began to take the children to church on a consistent basis. Sometimes, we attended the local Catholic church because it was easier with my work schedule. I just wanted to make sure that we were attending church. Unfortunately, going to church was the only thing we were doing. I wasn't learning and applying anything that I was hearing. While I was not actively looking for love this time, I jumped at the opportunity when someone from my past resurfaced. When that didn't work out, I found myself on dating sites because I didn't want to be alone. There I was doing it again. I was looking for love instead of allowing God's love to heal me. After several years of failed relationships and situationships, I found myself broken, in deep hurt, and feeling unloved even by God.

I was attending church regularly at that time. I was doing my best to stay above ground. The last relationship that ended, albeit a short one, brought me to my knees as I watched a webinar of a young unmarried woman discussing her relationships and triggers. Everything she said that night resonated with everything that I had gone through, searching for a love that no one person could provide. It was in that moment, on that floor, that I truly gave my life to Christ and felt His presence immediately. Most of all, I felt His love! It was the love that I had been literally searching for. That was the end of August 2018.

After that moment, I began to build a relationship with God. I began to learn more about Him by reading the Bible, going to Bible study when I could, and joining an online Christian community that supported biblical beliefs. I gained friendships that helped me to see my worth and who God designed me to be. In the first year, I intentionally did not date because I wanted to have a real foundation of love with the Father. I worked on me and healed. While I'm still working on healing in different areas of my life, I now know what real love looks like. My reference point of love is no longer a television show or romantic fairytale. My reference for love is God.

Throughout my 43 years, I was looking for a love that was already there. Every time He woke me up, that was love. Every time He protected me from my foolish decisions, that was love. Every time He severed relationships that would only harm me, that was love. The love that I was searching for was the Father's love for me. Once I recognized His love, I began to love myself and give me permission to love and be loved again. I am no longer afraid of the love that awaits me in the future. I am no longer afraid of getting hurt. I am no longer searching for love but allowing God to shower me with His love. When the time comes, I will be ready for the love of a lifetime.

Allow God to heal your heart. Allow Him to touch the parts of you that you fear someone will break because you've been broken so many times before. Allow Him to show you His love, so that you may love again. Remember this scripture.

> *[1Co 13:13 NLT] 13 Three things will last forever--faith, hope, and love--and the greatest of these is love.*

REFLECTION

Chapter Seven
IT'S OKAY TO LIVE

LIVE. The word appears in the King James Version of the Bible 766 times. If that doesn't get your attention, I'm sure the various definitions according to Webster's 1913 online dictionary will.

- To be alive; to have life; to have, as an animal or a plant, the capacity of assimilating matter as food, and to be dependent on such assimilation for a continuance of existence; as, animals and plants that *live* to a great age are long in reaching maturity.
- To pass one's time; to pass life or time in a certain manner, as to habits, conduct, or circumstances
- To make one's abiding place or home; to abide; to dwell; to reside.
- To be or continue in existence; to exist; to remain; to be permanent; to last
- To enjoy or make the most of life; to be in a state of happiness.
- To feed, to subsist; to be nourished or supported
- To have a spiritual existence; to be quickened, nourished, and actuated by divine influence or faith
- To be maintained in life; to acquire a livelihood; to subsist
- To outlast danger, to float

When trials and tribulations happen in our lives, we tend to shut down. We stop living our lives, trying to avoid the things of the past that hurt us. We stop passing time doing the things we love. We stop enjoying and making the most of life. We even cease to have a spiritual existence at times. When we are completely broken, we don't outlast danger. In fact, we run to it. We forget to fight for the very gift God has given us. Life.

I'm guilty of it all, even contemplating taking my life. Everything that happened to me prompted me to make "adjustments" in my life. I thought that if I stopped crying, life would be better. I thought that if I stopped feeling, life would be better. If I tried to be like the others and blend into the crowd, life would be better. If I didn't grieve and tried to be strong, life would be better. If I never fell in love again, life would be better. What I didn't realize was that the adjustments I made in my life were just prolonging the healing process and stealing time.

Years were passing by as one thing after another happened. Each time as I tried to protect myself, I backed myself into a corner and created a protective shell around my heart. It was like my heart was in Fort Knox with multiple fortified barriers surrounding it. While that may sound like the perfect solution to heartache, unfortunately, I blocked the One who created me from having access to my heart as well. This meant that I was rejecting the God I claimed to know and serve. How about that? The root of my issues was rejection. I was doing the same thing to God that I felt was being done to me. Oh, how I thank God that He is merciful, loving, and forgiving.

> [Jhn 10:10 KJV] 10 The thief cometh not, but for to steal, and to kill, and to destroy: I am come that they might have life, and that they might have [it] more abundantly.

This verse reminds me that Jesus gives me an abundant life that I choose to live.

Have you ever wondered why God would give us so many emotions? I did. After being on an extended emotional rollercoaster recently, I simply asked my Father why I am so emotional. His answer was so simple, yet so complex. He said that my emotions let me know that I am still living. Your emotions are indicators that you are the human being that God created in His image and in all His likeness. You feel what He feels. When you spend time with Him, you can even hear the things on His heart. That's the type of relationship He wants with us. Through prayer and reading His word, we learn the secrets of His heart. I can guarantee you that when you seek Him, you will feel His very breathe within you that gives life, new life.

> [Eze 36:26 KJV] 26 A new heart also will I give you, and a new spirit will I put within you: and I will take away the stony heart out of your flesh, and I will give you a heart of flesh.

When we accept Christ and allow God to give us a new heart and a new spirit, we begin to live a new life. Walking in the new life isn't always easy. Our old life (old flesh) often tries to pull us back to who we used to be before the spiritual heart transplant. After being baptized in December 2018 with my son, my entire life and lifestyle changed. I no longer desired to do many of the things I did before. I began to see everything differently. If you've ever heard the story of Paul and the scales falling from his eyes, imagine that experience. Walking with and living like Christ required me to begin to see things from a spiritual point of view. God began to show me movies and shows that I could no longer watch as well as music that I could no longer listen to. Don't misunderstand. I didn't become perfect suddenly. However, God showed me the way He wanted me to live. It was a struggle at first as I went from one extreme to the other. I went from being the woman who drank daiquiris with family and friends to the woman who didn't desire the taste of any alcoholic beverage. I went from watching movies that included a lot of cussing and sex scenes to feeling uncomfortable any time I tried to watch those same movies. I didn't do these things because I was trying to be better than anyone else or be "holier than thou." I simply obeyed God and began to implement the changes He desired for me. My desires became His desires. Because of Him, I was now living a new life based on His original design.

It wasn't an easy transition, and it is still ongoing. I remember celebrating New Year's Eve with friends the day after being baptized. One of my close friends decided to have a party at her house. I put on a dress that I didn't wear often. Dressing up wasn't really something I did unless I was attending a wedding or some other special occasion. I remember driving to her house and telling myself that I wasn't going to drink. Well, that went out the window. I don't remember getting drunk because I did drive home that night. However, I do remember a night of drinking and dancing. I remember an uncomfortable feeling that came over me which I ignored. I just wanted to have fun with my friends as I always did.

The next day I felt awful about how the night went. I was convicted. It's important to note that convicted is different from condemned. Conviction is recognizing that you've done something wrong and repenting for it. Condemnation is that same recognition attached to shame and self-hate. The events that happened that night were not the things that convicted me. Conviction came when I realized that I disobeyed Holy Spirit. That feeling of being uncomfortable was Holy Spirit telling me to call it a night and go home early. I had just accepted Christ as my Lord and Savior in front of everyone at my church the day before. Don't get me wrong, drinking alcohol is not a sin. Getting drunk is the actual sin. That's another topic for a later date. However, Holy Spirit prompted me not to drink and I disobeyed. It was disobedience that was my sin. I realized the next day that I must live for Christ in everything that I do.

Living for Christ can seem hard. Every Christian will tell you that the journey of living for Jesus Christ truly never ends. We are constantly renewing our minds in Him so that we don't go back to the old us. The truth is that living for Christ is about relationship. Just like any other relationship, there are things that we do that are pleasing to the other person. For example, if you know your wife loves flowers, you buy her flowers from time to time. In the same way, I honor God with my choices. It's my choice to live a Kingdom life that pleases Him. It's choosing to display the fruits of the Spirit in my words, thoughts, and actions because I am a representation of God and His love. Living the Kingdom life isn't about being an uptight, judgmental person dictating the choices of others as many might think. It's more about displaying His grace, love, and mercy so that you may walk in faith, hope, and love.

Jesus came so that we may live a more abundant life. He didn't intend for us to just exist. Just as He is alive in us, He intended for us to live full and fruitful lives. That type of life doesn't occur by just existing. That type of life happens when you step out on faith and go after the things that God has in store for you. Scripture refers to Abram moving to a place God showed him. It was this type of faith that led me to move to the small town that God literally showed me.

While going through one of the most trying times of my life, I realized that I had to rely on God more than anyone or anything. That required faith. So, after losing my job during the Covid pandemic, I took a leap of faith. I let go of my lease, knowing that I would have to find another place to live without a job. I remember the apartment complex asking for my new address when I gave my notice to vacate the apartment. I cried and laughed at the same time. I could only say, "I don't have a new address yet." That was the truth and all I could offer. True living and not just existing is living in Him. It's allowing Him to lead you where you should go even when the path is not clear to you. I have learned to follow Him in faith over this past year. The best part about this journey has been that God showed me that He is a man of His word. He said He would provide for me, and He did just that. During my 7 months of unemployment, every bill was paid on time or in advance. I applied for an apartment in a new city without a job and was approved. Can you say Provider? I still sit in awe at how He worked everything out. To sweeten the pot, I walked into the local pharmacy to buy vitamins and ended up with a job. Look at God!!

I said all of that just to say that living life is about taking steps in faith even when it doesn't look right. It's about trusting God with you heard Him say to do. It's about believing what He says about you. Living is not just waking up every day going through the motions. I've been there and done that. I was becoming robotic in everything just to escape the emotions. That's not the life that God wants us to live.

This book has been about all the things that we do to avoid the very emotions that God gives us so that we feel and live life to the fullest. He doesn't want us to become our emotions, but simply utilize them in the moment and breakthrough. As we continue to acknowledge and confront our emotions, we are empowered by God to turn the things that were meant to break us into stories of triumph. Those stories eventually help others to gain their breakthrough in Him. I pray that my testimonies lead you to seek Him with all that you are and embrace the feelings and emotions He gave you. Don't be afraid of life and the trials that come with it. Know that God is truly with you every step of the way.

> *[Jos 1:9 NLT] 9 This is my command--be strong and courageous! Do not be afraid or discouraged. For the LORD your God is with you wherever you go."*

REFLECTION

www.ingramcontent.com/pod-product-compliance
Lightning Source LLC
Chambersburg PA
CBHW071845290426
44109CB00017B/1935